CONTENTS

INTRODUCTION

If you're ever on YouTube, chances are that you have come across a video or two where the creator chimes in with: "This video is sponsored by..." before jumping into their regular content. You may have wondered why this is necessary. Perhaps you felt annoyed by the interruption. You may also have pondered over how your favorite YouTuber got a company to sponsor them in the first place or what they even gain from a sponsorship. Well, we're here to answer all of your questions regarding YouTube sponsorships.

SETTING UP A SPONSORSHIP

A sponsorship is when a company will pay you a flat rate to have an ad slot within your content to promote their products or their brand. How it works is a company will reach out to either you or your manager, or you can reach out to a company yourself. However, it is much more preferable to have a brand reach out to you because they already have a budget and are actively looking for influencers to sponsor.

Here are some well-known companies that sponsor a lot of YouTube content:

- Dollar Shave Club
- Skillshare
- SeatGeek
- Honey
- Audible
- NordVPN

"When people think of YouTube sponsors, they tend to think of large channels like Logan Paul and Pew-DiePie, but that's not always the case. Lucrative sponsorships for small YouTubers are possible too, it's just a matter of knowing how to do it."

Once you have connected with a potential sponsor, the next part to deal with is the negotiating and planning process. What you'll be doing during this process is talking about the price, what is included in the price, like the "deliverables," which are the actual physical products themselves that will get sent to you, and what type of content you'll be required to create, whether it's YouTube videos, Instagram stories and posts or making TikToks.

Once everything is agreed upon, a contract will be written up and signed. Before signing the contract, make sure you review it carefully just in case there's something there that you don't agree with and want changed. It can take a few weeks or even months to actually agree on the terms of a sponsorship, so this part of the process might not be all that pleasant, especially if you do not have a management team. However, in the end you'll know what you're looking for in future sponsorships and have strong relationships with brands.

CREATING SPONSORED CONTENT

When creating sponsored content, you cannot just dive into it right away, as some people may seem to believe. In reality, you have to come up with a concept and get it approved by the brand before you do anything else. A good tip for YouTubers just starting out is to shape your video ideas around what the brand that's sponsoring you stands for. This way, your videos will run more smoothly. For instance, if you are being sponsored by a skincare brand, it wouldn't make sense to incorporate them into a video about financial tips and tricks. The two topics aren't really related to one another.

"Sponsors want to know that you share their values and that your branding aligns with theirs. Unclear or mixed branding will harm a company's brand, so don't expect to gain a sponsorship if you don't know exactly who you are and why you do what you do."

Sellfy.com

When pitching ideas to the company, you'll want to make a rough outline of how the video is going to go. As the concept starts to develop into a more solid shape, you'll most likely work together with the brand to wrap up on the finishing touches. You and your sponsor will also determine the amount of time you talk about the brand in your video, whether it's merely a brief one-minute mention or a five-minute discussion. Typically, a brand will give you a list of talking points that they want you to acknowledge. They may even tell you what they don't want you to talk about.

GETTING YOUR CONTENT APPROVED

The whole process of sponsorships may take longer than you initially think. With sponsorships, it is best if you plan out your content ahead of time. This way, you'll be sure to give yourself enough time to go through the review process. It is recommended that you film your video a couple of weeks before the time that it is scheduled to go live. If you have to make some changes or edits to your video, you'll have the time to do so. To re-iterate, it is very important that you map out a timeline and have a content calendar. You do not want to miss an upload because a sponsored video did not get approved in time.

After you have finished creating your video, you'll want to make it clear that this video is being sponsored, for example, adding a disclaimer into the description box. Then, if you have a management team, you'll send the final draft to them, and they'll send it to the company.

HOW MUCH DO YOUTUBE SPONSORS PAY?

As there is quite a bit of negotiation involved with landing a sponsorship, there is no definitive answer to the exact amount that YouTube sponsors pay. For sponsored mentions, which are the most common types of sponsorships, the starting price is typically $20 to $30 per 1000 views. This is a considerable increase for YouTubers since the average payout for just simply running unskippable ads on their videos is only $2 to $8 per 1000 views.

It's understandable why creators would want to work with brands. But why do brands want to work with YouTubers? It's because viewers usually ignore the typical ad, but coming from an influencer, someone who they admire and respect, the message that the brand wants to get out will be more impactful coming from a content creator rather than a faceless company. That is why brands are willing to pay more for a YouTuber or other influencer to sponsor their products.

There is much more that goes into the process of sponsorships, but hopefully this information at least helps you get your foot in the door to begin your own YouTube journey.

SPONSORSHIP RULES
FOR EVERYONE

When offering influencer's sponsorships, brands have to adhere to Youtube and the Federal Trade Commission's policies. Part of the FTC's job is to protect consumers and they do this by stopping unfair, deceptive, and/ or fraudulent business practices by collecting reports from consumers while also conducting investigations. One of the policies brands have to adhere to is copyright infringement. This is defined as, "when a copyrighted work is reproduced, distributed, performed, publicly displayed, or made into a derivative work without the permission of the copyright owner".

This policy applies to both Youtubers and brands. If a video a brand has sponsored has copyrighted material in it like music, audio, video, or images that the Youtuber has not been given permission to use, the brand could be left vulnerable to legal troubles to fix the issue. Until the issue is resolved, the video has to be taken down and viewers will not be exposed to the brand, which could lose them money. Brands also have to be diligent about making sure that whatever they want the Youtuber they are sponsoring to do complies with the Youtube Terms of Service. The Youtube Terms of Service include protecting the community from harmful content, protecting copyrighted content, the monetization policies, and complying with local law. Brands also have to be in compliance with content commercial usage rights, which are requirements for brands for any uses that could make them money. The brand has to have the legal right by contract, patent, copyright, trademark, or agreement to make or sell a product in any country. So, whatever a brand wants a Youtuber to use in a sponsored video has to adhere to the content commercial usage rights.

HOW TO ATTRACT SPONSORS

If you're a Youtuber, try the platform Famebit to look for sponsorships. This platform is especially helpful for small channels. Famebit is an interface for brands advertising themselves and video creators looking for sponsorship for their content. Reaching out directly to brands for sponsorships is not the best method in which to get them, but it is definitely still an option. When reaching out, send brands a link to your channel so they can see how your content relates to whatever service or product they sell. Sending a link will also show them how different you are from other content creators. You want to show brands why they should choose you instead of the thousands of Youtubers who are most likely already reaching out to them.

Study the brand you want the sponsorship from and try to include any research you found into the reason why you want a partnership. Remember to personalize all the emails you send to brands. It probably won't be very effective to send the same email to 10 different brands, who all do different things, and expect success with most of them. You can also get sponsorships by going to Youtuber or content creator gatherings like VidCon. Here, you can meet brands looking for all types of Youtubers to sponsor. You can talk to representatives face-to-face and show them how you interact with your subscribers so they'll be excited about sponsoring you. Inspiring audience engagement can also attract sponsors to your channel. When sponsors see you have a dedicated audience, even if it's small compared to more popular influencers, they are motivated to work with you because they know you have sub-scribers who will most likely try a product that you recommend to them.

Strong branding will also bring sponsors to your channel. Define what your channel is about. What are the narrative or core values? What is your niche, what do you want to be known for, and what makes you unique? Constantly work with your brand image. You can do this by working on the look of your actual channel. Are you using bright colors and interesting pictures to capture the attention of your subscribers or any sponsors on your page? It's important to work on an interesting logo, maybe even a new one every few years. Lastly, establish a brand persona. What is the personality or attitude of your channel and content? What are you and your channel known for? Maintaining the same look with your clothes, your background, even the font style in your videos will make you look professional because you and your channel are easily recognizable. Your professionalism will draw sponsors to you and as well as consistent viewers who will see your sponsored video.

If you want to get the attention of a specific brand, try these methods. Have one of their products in the background of one of your videos, mention how much you love the product or service they provide, or include yourself using it. You can do this before they even reach out to show them and other brands you represent them and promote items well. This also shows any brands coming to your channel that you know promote, demonstrate, and sell a product effectively. For example, if you post a video promoting an app that helps you plan your day and incorporate it into your video about your day and nighttime routine, brands will see you know how to include conversation about the sponsorship into your regular content. As mentioned before, keeping your consist-ency is important. Sponsors are looking to see if all your videos are consistent in topic or niche and in posting the actual content.

You can also write a sponsorship letter, which is your effort to secure a deal or funding from the sponsor of your choice. It's important to personalize the letter for the sponsor you're writing to instead of sending every sponsor the same generic letter. Find a contact or a specific name of the person who handles sponsorships and address your letter to them personally. It will make you look even more invested in a partnership with them because you took the time to find these specific details. In the body of the letter, you can talk about yourself, but not for long. Make sure you talk about why you want them to sponsor you. You can do this by complimenting them, telling them what you like about their brand or company, and how their brand relates to what you do on your channel. Try to keep them short as well because sponsors do not want to read multiple pages to be convinced to take a chance on you with a deal.

Sponsors also don't want to see logos or other brands in videos that they are sponsoring. even if it is unintentional. This means that if a sponsor has chosen to do content with you, they don't want any other indications of brands and companies in that content. For example, cover up the HP symbol on your laptop in your sponsored video about the best treats for your new kitten. Be careful what other products you have in a view of the camera, even though they may seem irrelevant to the content you're filming.

QUESTIONS TO ASK YOURSELF

Before you look for sponsors, ask yourself why you want them. Whether you have a channel with a small or huge following, what about sponsorship makes you want to be a part of it? Next, ask yourself how sponsorship deals will affect your income strategy. Your income strategy is how and where you receive income. Lastly, ask yourself what unique qualities do you bring to the table besides your videos? Do you think you're convincing enough when promoting anything? When you watch your video back, would you try out a product or service on your own recommendation? Can you explain or demonstrate the use of a product well? These are important questions to consider when entering into a sponsorship deal because the brand that chose you is depending on the collaboration with you to make them money. You want to show brands you're worth choosing over millions of other youtubers.

HOW TO FIGURE OUT HOW MUCH TO CHARGE

There's actual math that you can apply to discover how much you are worth when it comes to being paid for sponsorships. The first step is to analyze your last 10 videos, secondly write down the number of views each video has received and add the 10 numbers up. Then divide the sum by 10 and you have your average video views. Once you have your average views, you can do research to discover how much is customary for your average video views so you know your worth and get paid by sponsorships accordingly. Reach out to other channels and ask them (if they feel comfortable volunteering that information) what they were paid for their sponsorships and that should help you get a good idea of what you should expect or ask for.

SPONSORSHIPS FOR SMALL CHANNELS

Before you enter into a sponsorship with any brand, get a good understanding of your analytics. This is the date that represents which videos get the most "traffic" or attention from viewers, how many views you have altogether or separately, and which videos get the most comments. So when the brand approaches you for this information, you know it well and they can use it to make decisions about your deal. To secure a sponsorship, you should probably have at least 1000 subscribers. Today that constitutes a small channel and it shows sponsors you're dedicated to posting content for an audience who's return you encourage. That many people also shows sponsors that you have enough content for them to look at to see if you're the right fit. You can also get sponsors if you have fewer than 1000 subscribers and another medium with a following, like a blog or an Instagram page with thousands of followers. The other exception is if you have high engagement. You may have just 500 subscribers to your channel, but many comments under each video or 500 or more people join when you go live. Sponsors do look for consistency, but they also like to see you experimenting with different kinds of content to see what your viewers like best.

PLATFORMS THAT CONNECT YOUTUBERS AND SPONSORS

There are countless platforms and websites that help connect content creators with sponsors. These platforms make it easier for sponsors to reach out to you because most of your information and a link to your channel will be there so they do not have to search for you. Among these platforms are Heepsy, Upfluence, and Aspire IQ. There are 11 million influencers or content creators on Heepsy with 500,000 or more subscribers. Brands can filter their search for Youtubers by category and location, audience filters, engagement rate, and outreach. Because of the 500,000 subscribers or more rule, smaller Youtubers won't have the chance to be found on Heepsy, but this a great platform for brands to find content creators they would have probably not found just searching the internet. Brands on Heepsy can also analyze the Youtuber's audience by authenticity score, demographics, cost estimations, and brand collaborations. An authenticity score is an individual's reported sense of authenticity or realness. This can also include if the Youtuber's viewers feel this way about them as well. Heepsy is a very helpful platform because brands can work with Youtubers they want according to their specific criteria.

Upfluence is a similar platform. It is a huge database of influencers for brands to choose from using specific criteria like Heepsy. Once a brand finds the right fit, they have your basic information like your email to contact you and set up the sponsorship. Aspire IQ does the same. Their criteria is aesthetic, location, and engagement metrics for brands to search by. Brands can also receive offers from influences who are interested in working with them. For brands, the platform offers a feature where it will communicate for them. It'll reach out to influencers to get details on when they'll be posting the sponsored content, send contract forms, and help with product management. There are countless other websites and platforms that help influencers secure brands and brands find fitting Youtubers.

Grapevine allows you as Youtuber to pick from a list of products that could fit your channel. Once you choose one, you can go about the process of contacting them to secure a sponsorship. Channel Pages also connects brands and Youtubers. You can create a profile for free and you don't have to have a certain number of subscribers. You can even tell them what kind sponsorships you're after so you can mold the choices you are shown

Tinysponsor is like other platforms in that it's a connection service and both brands and creators can be on it. Creators can build packages that are unique to them to offer to brands seeking deals. Packages can include prices and what the creator prefers to do with sponsorships, like if they'll center the entire video around a product or just dedicate five minutes to talking about it, if they're willing to buy the product themselves to try it out, or what kind of deals they prefer like promoting a product in exchange for it for free instead of money. Brands, businesses, and agencies can book the packages with creators and request custom packages. Sponsors can look for packages that best fit with what they're looking for, most likely depending on audience and goals.

Makrwatch is for both creators and YouTubers to connect. They want to create reliable revenue for creators so they can easily focus on investing in their channel and building it in a positive direction. Many who have used it say they provide consistent sponsorships and that Makrwatch is reliable. When you enter into a sponsorship, you can check the status of your payments and check for new sponsorship offers. They pride themselves in their efficient communication and constant help that allow creators to focus on making their content the best it can be without worrying about where their income is going to come from next.

PROGRAMS THAT OFFER SPONSORSHIPS

There are websites and programs that give content creators sponsorships of all kinds instead of connecting creators with brands that offer the sponsorships. One of these websites is the Razer Affiliate Program. With Razer, you can refer your subscribers to the website with banners and links on in your videos and in the description. Once a subscriber or viewer on your channel buys a product from Razor when they click on a link or banner on your video, you could get up to 10% commission. Sites like Razor are free to join, you get paid for every sale that's made through the links on your page, Razer gives you all banners and text links in all sizes, and anyone who is 18 is eligible to apply. There are many websites that work this same way and even though affiliate links are not traditional sponsorships, they're ways for Youtubers to get acquainted with the process. Although, beware these websites since most of them are for gaming. For gaming channels, these are amazing opportunities.

WHAT YOUTUBERS SHOULD NOT DO WHEN IT COMES TO SPONSORSHIPS

If you have a smaller YouTube channel, be cautious about the deals that are offered to you by brands. A fair amount of the time, brands will approach smaller channels with sponsorship deals because bigger channels have said no. The deal most likely is not beneficial for anyone, so they go to small channels because they assume they will be desperate for deals, views, and any kind of income. So make sure the deal you're being offered is good for you because some brands may try to get you to promote their product, service, and give you nothing for it. If you do have a respectable offer, make sure whatever brand it is fits with the image and topic of your channel so you prioritize your channel's theme and the sponsorship with the brand. There's nothing wrong with introducing a product or service people may be unaware of, but the brand can't be so unknown that nobody would search for your videos or watch it when you post it. Or your viewers may not appreciate that you are being sponsored by a brand that has nothing to do with what you do on your channel. For example, viewers may not be consistent with their support if you're a makeup channel and you're interrupting your festival makeup video to talk for three minutes about a new family board game. Your viewers come to your channel for not only your content, but new products or services that have to do with the topic of your channel.

Something you should definitely not do as a Youtuber is not disclose that you are being paid revenue apart from the regular revenue you get from ads or views. If viewers feel like you're hiding the fact you're being sponsored, that might turn them away. Posting a sponsored video is nothing to hide, so it could definitely make your viewers question you or become suspicious of you. Put that it's sponsored in both the description of the video and of course, the video itself. When you get a deal or simply accept an offer, don't get ahead of yourself and start making sponsored content before the deal is set in stone. Also, don't disrupt your regularly scheduled videos or planning schedule to start making the sponsored content. If you regularly post on Tuesday, don't post on Wednesday just to get the sponsored content out. Stay consistent and make sure your videos stay polished, professional, and interesting to watch as they've always been. Don't leave your work unfinished. This may seem obvious, but special care should be taken to make sure you don't leave the sponsored content unfinished, posted late, or missing information that the brand asked you to include. It can be hard to get sponsorships in the future if you have a reputation for not doing well on the opportunities you were given in the past. You can also miss out on the money you were meant to be paid if you don't do what you were asked to, or the brand will not react well to you being paid to meet their requests and you don't. This goes hand in hand with posting content the way you have agreed upon with the brand. Make sure all agreed-upon elements are there and it's posted on time according to your schedule or the brand's request.

WHAT BRANDS SHOULD DO

As a brand, try reaching out to smaller channels more instead of the gigantic channels with millions of subscribers. Trying this before you move on to bigger channels is wise because smaller channels have stronger connections with their subscribers since there are so few of them compared to the millions of people that watch, for example, PewDiePie's videos. There's more of a chance a smaller Youtuber has interacted with a good amount of their viewers and that personal connection will strengthen the probability of the viewers using the product. People are likely to buy a product or use a service because their friend or someone they trust recommends it and enjoys it.

TYPES OF SPONSORSHIPS

The first kind of sponsorships are the kind that offer money in exchange for you making the video or videos the brands have asked for. This is the simplest form of sponsorship and the deals that most Youtubers are offered. Next is affiliate links. This is when the Youtuber links the website of the manufacturer or brand and gets paid an agreed amount when a subscriber or a viewer clicks the link and buys the product. The payment is not direct like getting paid for videos, but the end result is the Youtuber still getting paid for using space in their video to promote the product or service at the request of the brand. The next is getting free products for businesses in exchange for you promoting it on your channel. With this, you can enjoy a free, potentially expensive product and the business gets the promotion. You don't get paid any money and it's kind of a one chance opportunity because once the product is yours, you only have to promote it once. Any time after the initial receipt of the free product is free promotion for the company without giving you anything more in return.

On a positive note, you can use the free product for as long as you want after you film the video. Be careful to only accept free products that you most likely would have bought anyway, otherwise you lose out on the deal. Whatever form or your sponsorship comes in, brands or companies and even the content creators themselves most likely offer packages. For example, the package you offer as the Youtuber could include a minute long spot in their video, a link in the description, a picture of the logo in the video, and a post on social media for a certain amount of money.

YOUTUBE SELECT

YouTube has created sponsorship opportunities in a program called YouTube Select. This allows brands to attach their promotions to themes on the platform, such as Black History Month or Mother's Day. Sponsorships become available on a quarterly basis with YouTube Select. Brands get the opportunity to tie into popular and have product or service promotions displayed with videos in a variety of categories. Along with YouTube Select, YouTube will offer other sponsorship opportunities. One of them is YouTube Greenlight. This enables brands to sponsor an original series from up-and-coming groups of content creators. Next is NFL Game Day Access, the chance to sponsor the show's episodes during regular and postseason. Lastly, there are seasonal event sponsorship opportunities like national holidays for marginalized groups. The platform has found ways to tie events in with chances for sponsorship for brands, which has and will give brands that maybe didn't have the chance to enter into sponsorship deals on the app.

WHAT VIDEOS CAN'T BE SPONSORED

ny videos that feature content with illegal products or services, pornography, sex or escort service, recreational drugs, mail order brides, pharmaceuticals without a prescription, unreviewed online gambling sites, explosives, hacking, phishing, or spyware, services to cheat on tests or exams, or misleading businesses. These types of videos most likely will be taken off of YouTube entirely, but if the content you make is along these lines, you will most likely never receive a sponsorship. Most brands will not want to enter into deals with you if that's the kind of content you regularly focus on, but even if they did, YouTube itself will not let you receive any kind of income from these videos. So be mindful of your decisions as a creator or be satisfied with never or rarely getting sponsorships from brands.

SMART TIPS

Negotiating in general is a good tip but negotiating a sponsorship deal over multiple videos is beneficial for both you and the brand. Brands sponsoring multiple videos can allow viewers to see them more than once so there's more of a chance of people patronizing them. As a Youtuber, you can get paid for multiple videos all at once instead of small amounts over time. This might seem obvious but get your deal in writing. Make sure all the details are sent to you, including how and when your payment will be made. If you do not get your sponsorship deal in writing, the brand could easily move on or not be interested in the partnership anymore and it will be easier for them to do so since there was no writing. Discover your worth so you know how much to ask for when discussing deals with brands. It's wise to know what is a fair amount of money to ask for because you do not want to be paid less than what you are worth for promoting.

YOU CAN LOSE SPONSORS, TOO

Scandals and controversies can hurt your relationships with sponsors. They can be so harmful that brands may sever all ties with you, even brands you've cultivated relationships with or have sponsored many of your videos. You could have 100 subscribers or 100,000, but your image could be harmed by any kind of controversy and any sponsors you have can easily withdraw their partnership because they do not want to be associated with a negative situation. Popular vlogger and leader of YouTube's VlogSquad David Dobrik has experienced this recently. A past member of his group of creator friends claimed he was forced to participate in activities he did not consent to and many of Dobrik's sponsors immediately ended their partnerships. He had standing sponsorships with many brands and lost them because of this allegation and will most likely never get them back. This scandal or any creator's make it difficult to secure any sponsorships in the future. So be mindful of your public image, your behavior, what you say, and your interactions with others. Don't believe your personality is separate from the deals you make with sponsors because if they discover anything negative you've said, done, or recorded, that will be their reason for ending their partnership with you.

The Pewdiepie Sponsorship Scandals

Felix Arvid Ulf Kjellberg (known on the internet as PewDiePie) is the highest subscribed Youtuber. He experienced the trouble you can get into if you don't approach sponsorships currently or claim to be sponsored when you aren't, as was Kjelberg's case. In 2017, the Youtuber posted a video with the title "Sponsored by Volvo " and stated in the video that it was sponsored by the car company "full disclosure". Volvo released a statement saying they did not have a partnership of any kind with the Youtuber. After statements from Volvo representatives, PewDiePie changed the title of the video "Sponsored by Saab," another car company that he did not have any partnerships with. It was thought that he lied to gain favor with other brands or companies because having a partnership makes a creator look desirable. Because of this scandal, other companies have refused to work with him, regardless of his superstar status on YouTube.

Youtubers cannot claim a sponsorship with a brand they have never worked with or even spoken with. You have to go through proper channels and reach out for sponsorships the professional way to avoid getting caught in a scandal that could have a negative effect on your subscriber count, the relationship you build with your viewers, and any relationships with sponsors in the future.

Before this scandal, Kjelberg was involved in another where he did not adequately disclose a sponsorship with WB Games in 2016. He did disclose that was being paid for the content, but only in the description box of the video. According to the FTC, this was deceptive and the Youtuber went on to disclose his sponsorships more obviously. This was a lesson to PewDiePie and other content creators, who learned that putting your sponsorship disclosure in the description is not enough when it comes to this particular partnership. Many Youtubers decide to put the disclosure in the title of the video to avoid any confusion or accusations of deception.

In 2017, Kjelberg lost a sponsorship with Disney because of anti-semetic content in multiple videos. He had a partnership with a video production division called Maker Studio. In the main video in question, the Youtuber paid two men in India to hold up a sign with a very anti-semetic statement and claimed he did not think they would do it. He also claimed it was a joke. After the video was posted, this video and two others with insensitive imagery were taken down and Google took their ads from it, but other videos with anti-semetic content were left on his channel.

It Doesn't Have To Be Malicious

Some Youtubers make choices that do not have malicious or negative intentions but appear that way to their subscribers and sponsors. They post content without fully thinking about how it will look to the people that pay them to make the content. This was the case with the YouTube couple, Myka and James Stauffer. They adopted a 2-year-old boy from China who suffered from neurological issues and autism. After raising him for months, they re-homed him permanently because they struggled to raise a child with his specific needs. Playtex Baby, Danimals, Suave, Mattel/ Barbie, Fabletics, and Chili's all suspended their partnerships and sponsorships with Myka after this information surfaced. Myka made sponsored content for these companies with this child that she rehomed, and it was thought it was wrong of her to include him in sponsored content about his adoption when she would not keep him in the family. Although the Stauffers claim to not give him up with any hateful intentions, the decision to post this information cost them sponsors that have expressed that they will not sponsor or partner with them going forward.

THE RISKS

As helpful and positive as sponsorships can be, they also have risks. One of the risks is how difficult negotiating deals can be. You could possibly lose hundreds of dollars on a sponsorship deal if you don't negotiate your worth well. Maybe find a social media lawyer to help you figure out how much a creator in your specific position should be paid for sponsorship deals. Sponsorships can also be a legal risk if you have any errors. As previously stated, Youtubers must comply with the Truth In Advertising Law, which is the disclosure that you're earning money from the sales of the product you are promoting. Even if you do not leave out the disclosure intentionally, you could face a fine up to $50,000. You are also at risk of being held responsible if the product you are promoting doesn't turn out to be as great as you or the company has claimed. Again, try speaking with a social media lawyer before taking a sponsorship because you wouldn't want to be held responsible.

SPONSOR BLOCKERS

There aren't many, but there are programs and apps that block sponsored content for people who do not want to see it. Instead of giving up your favorite creators because you have no desire to see their sponsored content, the program will skip it. Some feel strongly about creators selling products on their channels and think it's inappropriate or annoying. People can download through links made available by the creators of these programs. It doesn't seem to be mainstream just yet, so if you want to block sponsored content, you'll have to risk downloading this from an unknown place.

Others want to block sponsors because they don't appreciate the advertisements and paid content being shown so close together. It feels disruptive to them and less authentic for the creator to allow their work to be interrupted with any sponsorship in order to "just" get paid. Some viewers want to feel that their favorite creator is making content for their enjoyment and for fun and not feel that money is their only concern. This is not realistic, of course, but subscribers still want to keep this mentality.

GAMING SPONSORSHIPS

There are many ways to get gaming sponsors, ways that are not available for Youtubers who do not have gaming channels. There are platforms and services that specifically connect gaming Youtubers to sponsors. Two of them are called Powerspike and Hello Gamers. Powerspike takes information about your channel, such as subscribers and overall views, to help sponsors with similar criteria find you. Hello Gamers matches more professional gamers and streamers with sponsors. The platform also manages connections like others do, meaning they make communication easier and neither parties have to constantly stay on top of it. Fairly Odd Streamers is a platform with hundreds of brands and businesses that are available for sponsorship and affiliate marketing deals. New brands are added often. This helpful platform is specifically for streamers on a variety of social media like Twitch, YouTube, Discord, and Facebook. With Fairly Odd Streamers, you can have the chance to be sponsored by Amazon, Fiverr, and GameStop.

There are also esports or gaming events where gaming Youtubers can network and meet sponsors. Research the sponsors you want to work with and plan on speaking with them at these events. Maybe even take cards to hand out while you're there. As a gamer, it's important to have specific information about your channel. Such as what is the maximum amount of views you receive, how many views you have overall, and your viewer engagement.

Gaming sponsors in particular want to ensure that their product will be seen and purchased. With the gaming and streaming community on YouTube, viewer engagement is everything, so sponsors want to know that it's strong.

HOW SPONSORSHIPS HELP YOU GET MORE SUBSCRIBERS

When your current subscribers see you have sponsored content, they'll most likely try whatever product you are promoting because they like you and trust you. Especially with smaller channels with a more close-knit community, subscribers will try something on your recommendation. They will also have a desire for you to succeed and help you continue making content for them to enjoy, so they'll buy through the links in order for you to be paid. Once your subscribers use the products or service and see for themselves it's good, they'll be encouraged to tell more people about your channel and their positive experience with your sponsored content. Then you'll find your number of subscribers increase, which could attract more sponsors to your channel. Encouraging engagement like commenting will show future sponsors that you have had success with past sponsorships. If your viewers leave comments about how great a certain product is and bring more business to the brand, this shows your next sponsor you know what you're doing.

REAL LIFE OR JUST ADVERTISING?

Many ask if the Youtubers are entering into sponsorship deals because they truly like the product or because they want to be paid no matter what the product is. Is your favorite comedy Youtuber promoting a new app because they truly love it or because they're being paid to promote it positively? Being paid a considerable amount of money is certainly a good incentive for promoting a product or service for a brand, but can subscribers trust that the product is actually good? A lot of Youtubers will ensure that a product is to their liking before they agree to promote it. If it's as simple as an app, they'll most likely download it and try it first before they agree to any deals. If it's an expensive product, they might take the chance to buy the product and test it because they don't want to tell their subscribers to buy something that does not work well or do what it advertises.

KIDS ARE PROTECTED, MOSTLY

If you're a Youtuber, you have to check a certain box to inform the platform that your video includes a sponsorship or a paid promotion. Once you make this known, your video will not be found on YouTube Kids so children cannot be exposed to it. Of course, kids on regular YouTube would not be shielded from these sponsorships, but YouTube Kids will always be a safe place for children against sponsorships. Kids are protected from sponsorships and most ads because they are a form of manipulation. They use psychology and in the case of kids, developmental psychology, to persuade children to ask their parents to purchase products for them. As well as this, a lot of videos aren't meant for kids to watch, so the products they promote aren't meant for kids either. For example, a youtuber that talks about the latest celebrity drama might promote an app that allows you to video chat with your friends, but most six- or seven-year-olds don't have much use for video chatting. So the video and the sponsorship could literally not make sense to them. The ad could also be for a product that they are too young to own, like a flat iron that gives its user the straightest hair.

Another reason ads are not permitted to be shown to children is because they are not aware they are being shown ads or sponsored content. Popular kids' Youtuber Ryan Kaji has faced this problem in the past. In 2019, a complaint was filed against Kaji (more likely his parents because they control his channel) because of his paid videos. Some videos were endorsed or sponsored by brands like Colgate, Hardee's, and Chuck E. Cheese. The complaint is arguing that the disclosures were not at all adequate or in language the preschoolers and young children that watch him could understand. On top of this, they have almost no way of figuring out what is sponsored and what is the actual video content because they are too young to know the difference between Ryan playing with new toys and promoting them. They don't understand Ryan gets paid to be on YouTube and that companies pay him apart from that in exchange for promotions. So they would not understand the disclosure. This, along with other events, violated the Children's Online Privacy Protection Act and brought on a $170 million fine YouTube was charged to pay. YouTube has become more vigilant about protecting children from ads and sponsored content, but young Youtubers like Kaji have been used to deceive children into wanting products.

SPONSORED CONTENT FOR TIKTOK

TikTok became the most popular social app in 2020. Naturally, sponsors transitioned there. For each view on sponsored content on TikTok, the creator gets paid 1 to 2 cents. For a creator with millions of followers and views on each video, 1 to 2 cents could amount to $10,000 for sponsored content. On YouTube, users can be paid 3 to 8 cents per sponsored view. The app is still considered new, so there's no standard price structure. The creator can also be paid a one-time fee for sponsored content so there's no danger of earning next to no money because you don't have many views or the algorithm does not push your video forward. Both platforms focus heavily on viewer engagement and sponsors are concerned the most about this when it comes to offering deals to creators. They want to see that your fans talk with you in the comments, that you have sponsored content already, and how likely your subscribers or followers would be to try a product on your recommendation.

SPONSORSHIPS ON INSTAGRAM

How to get sponsored on Instagram is similar to how to get sponsors on YouTube. First, you define your brand. What do you usually post? Family videos or pictures? Comedy? Fashion content? Secondly, know your audience. Do you post content more relatable to young mothers? Or sports fans? How old are they, what do they like to do that you do on your channel. Thirdly, post with consistency. Sponsors like to see they can rely on you to stick to schedule, as this is one indication of professionalism. Use hashtags to make your posts more discoverable and also geotags. Geotags allow your followers to know where you are. Since your opinion is important to them, they might visit the saem places you do. Don't forget to tag brands that sponsor you and promote them well. But before this, be sure to include contact information in your biography so brands that are interested know how to reach you. Like with other platforms, reach out to sponsors to discuss deals. This is a good way to establish your worth because you know the money you deserve; brands are more likely to give you that amount or around it. Don't forget to disclose the sponsorships in your captions.

FROM THE BRAND'S
POINT OF VIEW

When you're a part of a brand or a business and it's your job to reach out to influencers, create a timeline and plan for how exactly you're going to reach out. Try using timeline graphic programs to show your team or just yourself how you're going to do this. Planning will also help you give adequate time to each influencer or creator you reach out to. For example, you can plan to reach out to 20 creators in a two-month period. You can even have specific times and dates to contact these creators if that's better for you personally. You can keep the influencers that didn't answer in your rotation. Next, get a good understanding of your budget. If you have a $100,000 budget, you can decide how many people you want to spread over the budget. For example, do you want to offer $1,000 to 10 creators or a little over $300 to 30 creators. Thirdly, what's your business's target audience? The target audience correlates to what kind of Youtuber you'll be seeking. Create a profile for the kind of customers you'll be seeking so you can find Youtubers that fit the profile. You may sell gently used clothes for women under 3o, so you can find young female Youtubers that review clothes or focus on fashion.

The creator will most likely give you statistics when you reach out to them so you can get a better understanding of how their demographics fit with your business. When you start actually looking for specific Youtubers to reach out to, you can use resources to find

Youtubers based on any criteria you enter. You can discover their channel stats as well. When you narrow down your list, study the Youtubers you have chosen and reach out to. Beforehand, you want to make sure they're compatible with your business and remember that being compatible is more important than the Youtuber's popularity. When you enter into deals, negotiate, be specific about what you want, but also leave some room for the Youtuber's creativity.

TOOLS THAT HELP SPONSORSHIPS RUN SMOOTHLY AND HELP CREATORS

There are websites and programs that help brands and businesses conduct sponsorships easier. Youtubers can use these programs as well, but they're mostly for the purposes of the brands. The first is Venngage, an infographic design program. Among other things, Venngage helps the user create a timeline for their business projects. It also offers organizational charts and financial charts for you as the brand to stay organized while reaching out to several Youtubers at the same time. You can track how much you're offering each Youtuber and who's responded to your offers.

BuzzSumo is a platform that helps the users find the best content, opportunities, and engagement for you as a brand. It's an influencer finder and helps you connect with the influencer like other platforms. SocialBlade provides anyone with a public database of global information for any Youtuber, live streamer, or brand. You can see all data for creators and decide based on their channel's focus, their lifetime views, and their engagement. SocialBlade also helps Youtubers improve the quality of their videos and help make them better in multiple ways. You can learn how to build up your subscribers and increase interest in your channel. YouTube experts will look at your channel and give you tips on how to improve it. They'll take you step by step on how to do this as well. For brands and businesses, you can use SocialBlade's business API. An API is defined as, "public persona for an enterprise that exposes defined assets, data or services for consumption by a selected audience of developers" and they can be accessed by developers. The platform allows you to integrate it into your systems as well.

SOMETIMES THE SPONSORSHIP CAN BE RANDOM

Occasionally, the sponsorship may not have anything to do with what a YouTuber's channel is about. This is seen the most with creators that focus on food related content. Sponsors that focus on food do enter into deals with food creators, such as HelloFresh, the service that delivers ingredients and instructions to residences so people can make dinners easily. But some sponsorships for food creators can be skincare lines, workout apps or equipment, or big names like Amazon. Some YouTubers, food or not, find a way to incorporate their sponsor's product or service into their content. A creator could have such a specific niche that it's difficult to find sponsors that focus on their exact content area. For example, a creator that reviews technology will have lots of brands to choose from while looking for a sponsorship, but a creator that teaches viewers how to take care of exotic pets might have to branch out to other brands and tie in unrelated products. This is when a YouTuber's creativity becomes important because it is not easy to tie skincare into a video about their favorite vegetarian meals. It's difficult, but entirely possible.

SPONSORSHIP CALCULATORS

If you don't want to rely on other YouTubers to tell you what they usually get paid for internships because it differs from person to person, you can use a sponsorship calculator that tells you how much you should expect to be paid based on how many followers you have on a platform. This won't be exact because brands have specific budgets for their sponsorships, but this could be a fair estimate. Some sponsors offer larger amounts of money based on followers since they know more people will be likely to see the sponsored content and buy the product, earning them more money. Although it won't be exact, you'll have a good guess at what kind of money you can expect. Try multiple calculators to get all your possible price ranges. The prices differ on each social media platform, so a sponsored post on Snapchat probably won't cost the same as sponsored content on YouTube. But the calculators are good tools for either platforms or lots of others.

LGBTQ+ YOUTUBERS AND SEX EDUCATION SPONSORSHIPS

A good number of LGBTQ+ content creators have been sponsored by sex toy companies like Adam and Eve, but this content was not been well received by YouTube at first. Some YouTubers who make sex education content are a part of the LGBTQ+ community, so naturally they are sponsored by related products. In 2019, the platform issued warnings to You-Tubers who were sponsored by the sex toy company or had their links in their description boxes. 3 warnings or strikes against your channel will result it in being deleted and the sex educators feel that their channel is unfairly at risk just because of the topic of their channel, which cannot be monetized because of what they choose to focus on. Many creators had to return to past videos and delete the links from their description boxes in order to keep from being given another warning. If they decide to end any sponsor-ships they have with Adam and Eve or any other similar company, they are letting go of any income they could have had because they can't be paid by YouTube for their content.

MRBEAST'S SPONSORSHIPS

Jimmy Donaldson, known as MrBeast on YouTube, is the second highest creator on the platform. He is sponsored by many brands, but mostly by the popular coupon website Honey. He is also sponsored by Quibb, a network to share industry news and analysis. His sponsorships are just one of his forms of income and allow him to sustain his channel while working on other projects. Sponsorships do not have to be your only source of sufficient income as a Youtuber. Creators like MrBeast don't depend on sponsorships as much as creators with smaller channels and anyone can build up their channel popularity or side business to support them primarily like Donaldson does.

THE LUXURY LOOT SPONSORSHIP SCAM

YouTubers like Jake Paul and RiceGum were under criticism for being sponsored by and promoting a company called Mystery Brand, which is where users buy a mystery box that might hold merchandise worth hundreds or thousands of dollars. They both did videos unboxing the mystery boxes they spent thousands on and got to keep pricey items like AirPods and designer sneakers. Days after RiceGum's video sponsored by Mystery Brand, other creators began to call them out and say that this content was a bad idea to post because they are telling the children that follow them to pay hundreds of dollars for a possible luxury item. The videos were also received badly because the website has been reported to be a scam. Users who expected to receive luxury items were instead given fake versions. RiceGum apologized but reminded his fans that it's their responsibility to do research before they buy anything from anywhere.

Both RiceGum and Paul failed to mention that buyers could receive unbranded items as well as luxury items. The company also has a history of sending winners fake tracking numbers or simply not sending their packages after months of waiting. The art in the thumbnails of the videos are even stolen. They are the work of an artist named Alex Griendling, who says he is unsettled by the fact that his images are being used to coerce children into using a gambling website. Many are confused about why either Paul or RiceGum would even accept the sponsorship, since the highest amount they offer is $10,000 and compared to the money either of them usually make, this opportunity could have been passed on.

OTHER SPONSORSHIP LOSSES AND SCANDALS

Laura Lee, a YouTube makeup artist, lost several (if not all) of her sponsorships because of racist tweets she posted in 2012. On top of Ulta not releasing her line of beauty products, she lost her sponsorships with a sunglasses brand, Morphe Brushes, and a subscription service called BoxyCharm. Moon Bokhee, a popular YouTuber who eats in front of the camera for her fans, was accused in 2020 of hiding her sponsorships and not even eating the entirety of the food in her videos. Countless YouTubers have been caught accepting internships without disclosing them and leave many of their subscribers wondering why they think they need to hide their paid partnerships. When other sponsors see that you have not been truthful about your partnerships, they will be less likely to reach out to you to work with them.

MAKEUP SPONSORSHIPS

Like with other YouTubers, it's important to set up a Twitter and Instagram to stay connected with your subscribers. Building up your fanbase is important to sponsors who want to know their product will be seen by a good number of people. Be consistent with your content so you have information about channels and views to bring to sponsors. For makeup, good content would be reviews of makeup products, tutorials, and showcasing special looks like Halloween makeup. An important facet of being a beauty creator is making sure your content is helpful to people who want to get into doing makeup themselves. Start emailing makeup brands and companies when you're more established, which makeup companies prefer. Once you secure deals, follow the basic rules previously established. Disclose all sponsorships and fulfill all the requirements asked of you by the company.

Creators in the beauty community secure huge sponsorships. James Charles secured a sponsorship with CoverGirl that made history when they made him the first male brand ambassador. He reportedly earned $600,000 from this partnership. NikkieTutorials, the popular Dutch beauty YouTuber, had a sponsorship with Ofra Cosmetics, the cruelty free company. Manny MUA, one of the few male makeup artists on the platform, were sponsored by Maybelline, a popular brand that takes pride in their mascara. These are major national and even worldwide brands and being sponsored by them gains more fans or the attention of other popular

brands.

ALWAYS RESEARCH

When it comes to sponsorships, some YouTubers don't care who is sponsoring them as long as they get paid, but it's important to research the company first. Are their products reliable? Do they have good reviews? Have other YouTubers had good experiences with them? Are they good at communicating with you? Are they willing to negotiate? Do they offer good deals that benefit you as well as them? Do they have a history of scams? Unhappy customers? Bad deals or contracts with creators? Find out as much information as you can until you feel comfortable with what you know about the company and until you feel comfortable with working with them.

MARKIPLIER'S TAKIS SPONSORSHIP JOKE

Incidents with sponsors don't always have to be scandalous or career ending. The popular creator Mark Fischbach posted a sarcastic, joking video about how he was upset his favorite chip company, Takis, sponsored YouTuber Ninja and TikToker Charli D'Amelio but not him. He is crying in the video, holding a bag of chips and asking why he couldn't get a sponsorship from them. He claimed to be hurt and ended his relationship with the snack that he loves. He even said if they offered to sponsor him, he wouldn't even ask for money. Some even called it the worst breakup of the year and his fans found it hilarious, with no backlash from the Takis company. Content like this can actually attract sponsors as well because it tells the company that you are interested in working with them. Markiplier's or YouTuber's jokes could lead to sponsorships because dedicating an entire video to a brand who hasn't yet sponsored you sends a loud message to them that their partnership would be important to you. This goes hand in hand with the idea to have a product or service in a video that hasn't yet sponsored you to show them you are serious about working with them or that you are to conduct a sponsorship well.

AFTERWORD

Getting sponsors for your YouTube channel is not as difficult as it seems. Anyone, big or small, can find them. Smaller channels have to start out slowly and with less money than bigger ones, but it is possible. Whoever it is, research the companies or brand you reach out to or accept a deal from. Being paid is always great but be careful with who you go into business with. Get creative, stay consistent with your connection, keep it professional, and secure those sponsorships!